Ketogenic Crockpot I
By Don Orwell

http://SuperfoodsToday.com

Your Free Gift

As a way of saying thanks for your purchase, I'm offering you my FREE eBook that is exclusive to my book and blog readers.

Superfoods Cookbook - Book Two has over 70 Superfoods recipes and complements Superfoods Cookbook Book One and it contains Superfoods Salads, Superfoods Smoothies and Superfoods Deserts with ultra-healthy non-refined ingredients. All ingredients are 100% Superfoods.

It also contains Superfoods Reference book which is organized by Superfoods (more than 60 of them, with the list of their benefits), Superfoods spices, all vitamins, minerals and antioxidants. Superfoods Reference Book lists Superfoods that can help with 12 diseases and 9 types of cancer.

http://www.SuperfoodsToday.com/FREE

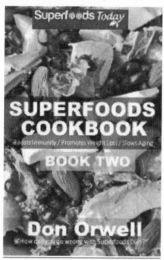

Table of Contents

Introduction

Hello,

My name is Don Orwell and my blog SuperfoodsToday.com is dedicated to Superfoods Lifestyle.

I hope that you will enjoy 100% Ketogenic Crockpot Superfoods recipes that I prepared for you. Don't be afraid of onions, carrots, red peppers and similar veggies in recipes because amounts for 6-8 people are 1 onion, 1 carrot, 1 red pepper etc. These veggies will improve the taste of dishes a lot, without adding a lot of carbs. One carrot, one onion and 1 red pepper have 20 net carbs in total, but since most of the recipes are for 8 servings, that makes it less than 3 carbs per serving. Enjoy!!

Ketogenic Superfoods Crockpot Recipes

Allergy labels: SF – Soy Free, GF – Gluten Free, DF – Dairy Free, EF – Egg Free, V - Vegan, NF – Nut Free

Broths

Some recipes require a cup or more of various broths, vegetable, beef or chicken broth. I usually cook the whole pot and freeze it in one cup or half a cup chunks.

Vegetable broth

Servings: 6 cups

Ingredients

- 1 tbsp. coconut oil
- 1 large onion, chopped
- 2 stalks celery, including some leaves
- 1 carrot, chopped
- 1 bunch green onions, chopped
- 8 cloves garlic, minced
- 8 sprigs fresh parsley
- 6 sprigs fresh thyme
- 2 bay leaves
- 1 tsp. salt
- 2 quarts water

Instructions - Allergies: SF, GF, DF, EF, V, NF

Put all ingredients in slow cooker and cook on low for 4 hours. Other ingredients to consider: broccoli stalk, celery root. Let cool to warm room temperature and strain. Keep chilled and use or freeze broth within a few days.

Chicken Broth

Ingredients

- 4 lbs. fresh chicken (wings, necks, backs, legs, bones)
- 2 peeled onions or 1 cup chopped leeks
- 2 celery stalks
- 1 carrot
- 8 black peppercorns
- 2 sprigs fresh thyme
- 2 sprigs fresh parsley
- 1 tsp. salt

Instructions - Allergies: SF, GF, DF, EF, NF

Put all ingredients in slow cooker and cook on low for 6 hours. Let cool to warm room temperature and strain. Keep chilled and use or freeze broth within a few days.

Beef Broth

Ingredients

- 4-5 pounds beef bones and few veal bones
- 1 pound of stew meat (chuck or flank steak) cut into 2-inch chunks
- Olive oil
- 1-2 medium onions, peeled and quartered
- 1-2 large carrots, cut into 1-2 inch segments
- 1 celery rib, cut into 1 inch segments
- 2-3 cloves of garlic, unpeeled
- Handful of parsley, stems and leaves
- 1-2 bay leaves
- 10 peppercorns

Instructions - Allergies: SF, GF, DF, EF, NF

Heat oven to 375°F. Rub olive oil over the stew meat pieces, carrots, and onions. Place stew meat or beef scraps, stock bones, carrots and onions in a large roasting pan. Roast in oven for about 45 minutes, turning everything half-way through the cooking.

Place everything from the oven in the slow cooker and cook on low for 6 hours. After cooking, remove the bones and vegetables from the pot. Strain the broth. Let cool to room temperature and then put in the refrigerator.

The fat will solidify once the broth has chilled. Discard the fat (or reuse it) and pour the broth into a jar and freeze it.

Curry Paste

This can be prepared in advance and frozen. There are several curry recipes that are using curry paste and I decided to take the curry paste recipe out and have it separately. So, when you see that the recipe is using curry paste, please go to this part of the book and prepare it from scratch or defrost of you have it frozen. Don't use processed curry pastes or curry powder; make it every time from scratch. Keep the spices in original form (seeds, pods), ground them just before making the curry paste. You can dry heat in the skillet cloves, cardamom, cumin and coriander and then crush them coarsely with mortar and pestle.

Ingredients

- 2 onions, minced
- 2 cloves garlic, minced
- 2 teaspoons fresh ginger root, finely chopped
- 6 whole cloves

- 2 cardamom pods
- 2 (2 inch) pieces cinnamon sticks, crushed
- 1 tsp. ground cumin
- 1 tsp. ground coriander
- 1 tsp. salt
- 1 tsp. ground cayenne pepper
- 1 tsp. ground turmeric

Instructions - Allergies: SF, GF, DF, EF, V, NF

Heat oil in a frying pan over medium heat and fry onions until transparent. Stir in garlic, cumin, ginger, cloves, cinnamon, coriander, salt, cayenne, and turmeric. Cook for 1 minute over medium heat, stirring constantly. At this point other curry ingredients should be added or let cook and freeze.

Soups

Bouillabaisse

Serves 6.

Ingredients - Allergies: SF, GF, DF, EF, NF

- 3 pounds of 3 different kinds of fish fillets
- 1/4 cup olive oil
- 1-2 pounds of Oysters, clams, or mussels
- 1 cup shrimp, crab, or lobster meat, or rock lobster tails
- 1 thinly sliced onion
- 2 cloves garlic, crushed
- 1 tomato, chopped
- 1 sweet red pepper, chopped
- 4 stalks celery, thinly sliced
- 2-inch slice of fennel or 1 tsp. of fennel seed
- 3 sprigs fresh thyme or 3/4 tsp. dried thyme
- 1 bay leaf
- 2-3 whole cloves
- 1/2 tsp. saffron
- 2 teaspoons salt
- 1/4 tsp. black pepper
- 3 cups fish broth
- 2 Tbsp. lemon juice

Instructions

Put all ingredients in the slow cooker and cook on low for 4 hours.

Italian Beef Soup

Serves 6

Ingredients - Allergies: SF, GF, DF, EF, NF

- 1 pound minced beef
- 1 clove garlic, minced
- 2 cups beef broth
- 1 tomato
- 1 sliced carrot
- 2 small zucchini, cubed
- 3 cups spinach - rinsed and torn
- 1/4 tsp. black pepper
- 1/4 tsp. salt

Put all ingredients in slow cooker and cook on low for 8 hours.

Avgolemono – Greek lemon chicken soup

Serves 4

Ingredients - Allergies: SF, GF, DF, EF, NF

- 4 cups chicken broth
- salt and pepper
- 3 eggs
- 3 tbsp. lemon juice
- Handful fresh dill (chopped)
- shredded roasted chicken (optional)

Whisk lemon juice and the eggs until smooth. Add about 1 cup of the hot broth into the egg/lemon mixture and whisk to combine.

Put all ingredients in the slow cooker and cook on low for 4 hours.

Ketogenic Minestrone

Serves 8-10

Ingredients - Allergies: SF, GF, DF, EF, NF

- 3 tbsp. olive oil
- 2 cloves garlic, chopped
- 1 small onion, chopped
- 3 cups chopped celery
- 1 carrot, sliced
- 2 cups chicken broth
- 2 cups water
- 2 cups broccoli
- 2 cups baby spinach, rinsed
- 1 zucchini, quartered and sliced
- 1 tbsp. chopped oregano
- 2 tbsp. chopped basil
- salt and pepper to taste

Instructions

Put all ingredients in the slow cooker and cook on low for 6 hours.

Cioppino

Serves 6

Ingredients - Allergies: SF, GF, DF, EF, NF

- 1/4 cup olive oil
- 1 onion, chopped
- 2 cloves garlic, minced
- 1 bunch fresh parsley, chopped
- 1 tomato
- 2 cups fish or vegetable broth
- 2 bay leaves
- 1 tbsp. dried basil
- 1/2 tsp. dried thyme
- 1/2 tsp. dried oregano
- 2 cups water
- 1-1/2 pounds peeled and deveined large shrimp
- 1-1/2 pounds bay scallops
- 18 small clams
- 18 cleaned and debearded mussels
- 1-1/2 cups crabmeat
- 1-1/2 pounds cod fillets, cubed

Instructions

Put all ingredients in the slow cooker and cook on low for 4 hours.

Chicken Winter Soup

Serves 6

Ingredients - Allergies: SF, GF, DF, EF, NF

- 2 pounds chicken pieces with skin on
- 1 clove garlic, minced, 1 Tbsp. minced ginger, 3 bay leaves
- 6 cups water
- ½ cup sliced parsley & ½ cup sliced cilantro
- 1 cup sliced carrots
- 2 cup sliced celery
- 1/4 cup sliced spring onions
- 1 sliced onion
- 1/4 tsp. black pepper
- 1/4 tsp. salt

Put all ingredients in slow cooker and cook on low for 8 hours.

Star Anise, Chicken & Leeks Soup

Serves 6

Ingredients - Allergies: SF, GF, DF, EF, NF

- 3 cups chicken broth
- 2 cups water
- 1 sliced carrot
- ½ cup sliced leeks
- 2 cups sliced celery
- 1 pound chicken
- 1/4 tsp. black pepper
- 4 star anise
- 1 clove garlic, minced, 1 Tbsp. minced ginger, 3 bay leaves
- 1/2 tsp. salt

Put all ingredients in slow cooker and cook on low for 8 hours.

Slow Cooker Recipes

Kale Pork

Serves 4

Ingredients - Allergies: SF, GF, DF, EF, NF

- 1 tbsp. coconut oil
- 1 pound pork tenderloin, trimmed and cut into 1-inch pieces
- 3/4 tsp. salt
- 1 onion, finely chopped
- 2 cloves garlic, minced
- 2 teaspoons paprika
- 1/4 tsp. crushed red pepper (optional)
- 4 cups chicken broth
- 1 bunch kale, chopped

Instructions

Put all ingredients in the slow cooker and cook on low for 4 hours.

Barbecued Beef

Serves 8

Ingredients - Allergies: SF, GF, DF, EF, NF

- 1 Tbsp. lemon juice
- 1 chopped carrot
- 2 tbsp. mustard
- 2 cups chopped celery
- 1/2 tsp. salt
- 1/4 tsp. black pepper
- 1/2 tsp. minced garlic
- 4 pounds boneless chuck roast

Instructions

Place chuck roast in a slow cooker. Pour all ingredients over and mix well. Cover, and cook on low for 7 to 9 hours.

Superfoods Goulash

Serves 4-6

Ingredients - Allergies: SF, GF, DF, EF, NF

- 3 cups cauliflower
- 2 pounds ground beef
- 1 small onion, chopped
- salt to taste
- black pepper to taste
- garlic to taste
- 1 Tbsp. paprika

Put all ingredients in the slow cooker and cook on low for 6 hours.

Chicken Cacciatore

Serves 8

Ingredients - Allergies: SF, GF, DF, EF, NF

- 4 pounds of chicken thighs, with skin on
- 2 Tbsp. extra virgin olive oil or avocado oil
- Salt
- 1 small sliced onion
- 1 sliced red or green bell pepper
- 8 ounces sliced cremini mushrooms
- 2 minced garlic cloves
- 1 peeled and chopped tomato
- 1/2 tsp. black pepper
- 1 tsp. dry oregano
- 1 tsp. dry thyme
- 1 sprig fresh rosemary
- 1 tbsp. fresh parsley
- 1 tsp. paprika

Instructions
Put all ingredients in the slow cooker and cook on low for 4 hours.

Cabbage Stewed with Meat

Serves 8

Ingredients - Allergies: SF, GF, DF, EF, NF

- 1-1/2 pounds ground beef
- 2 cups beef stock
- 1 small chopped onion
- 1 bay leaf
- 1/4 tsp. pepper
- 2 sliced celery ribs
- 4 cups shredded cabbage
- 1 carrot, sliced
- 1/4 tsp. salt

Instructions

Put all ingredients in the slow cooker and cook on low for 5 hours.

Green Chicken Stew

Serves 6-8

Ingredients - Allergies: SF, GF, DF, EF, NF

- 2 cups broccoli florets
- 1 cup chopped celery stalks
- 1/4 cup sliced leeks
- 2 tbsp. coconut oil
- 1/4 cups green peas (optional)
- 2 cups chicken stock
- 1/2 tsp. salt
- 1/4 tsp. black pepper
- 1/2 tsp. minced garlic
- 4 pounds boneless skinless chicken pieces

Instructions

Put all ingredients in the slow cooker and cook on low for 4 hours.

Irish Cauliflower Stew

Serves 8

Ingredients - Allergies: SF, GF, DF, EF, NF

- 1 small chopped onion
- 2 Tbsp. coconut oil
- 1 sprig dried thyme
- 2 1/2 pounds chopped meat from lamb neck
- 1 chopped carrot
- 2 cups cauliflower
- 5 cups chicken stock
- Salt
- Black pepper
- 1 bouquet garni (thyme, parsley and bay leaf)
- 1 bunch chopped parsley

Instructions

Put all ingredients in the slow cooker and cook on low for 6 hours.

Greek Beef Stew (Stifado)

Serves 8

Ingredients - Allergies: SF, GF, DF, EF, NF

- 4 large pieces of veal or beef osso bucco
- 4 whole shallots, peeled
- 3 bay leaves
- 3 garlic cloves
- 3 sprigs rosemary
- 6 whole pimento (optional)
- 5 whole cloves
- 1/2 tsp ground nutmeg
- 1/2 cup olive oil or avocado oil
- 1/3 cup apple cider vinegar
- 1 tbsp. salt
- 1/4 tsp black pepper

Instructions

Put all ingredients in the slow cooker and cook on low for 8 hours.

Beef, Parsnip, Celery Stew

Serves 8

Ingredients - Allergies: SF, GF, DF, EF, NF

- 2 1/2 pounds cubed beef meat
- 1 small chopped onion
- 1 chopped carrot
- 2 Tbsp. coconut oil
- 1 sprig dried thyme
- 1 small chopped parsnip (optional)
- 4 cups beef stock
- Salt
- Black pepper
- 1 bouquet garni (thyme, parsley and bay leaf)
- 1 bunch chopped parsley

Instructions

Put all ingredients in the slow cooker and cook on low for 8 hours.

Chicken Mushrooms & Olives Stew

Serves 6

Ingredients - Allergies: SF, GF, DF, EF, NF

- 4 pounds chicken with skin on
- 1 chopped carrot
- 1 small chopped onion
- 2 tbsp. coconut oil
- 2 cups sliced mushrooms
- 1 cup chopped celery
- 1/2 cup black olives
- 1/2 tsp. salt
- 1/4 tsp. black pepper
- 1/2 tsp. minced garlic
- ½ cup fresh parsley

Instructions

Put all ingredients in the crockpot, cover and cook on low 6 hours.

Osso Bucco & Garlic Stew

Serves 6-8

Ingredients - Allergies: SF, GF, DF, EF, NF

- 8 cloves garlic
- 1 small chopped onion
- 1 chopped carrot
- 2 cups chopped celery
- 2 tbsp. coconut oil
- 2 cups beef stock
- 1/2 tsp. salt
- 1/4 tsp. black pepper
- 1 tsp. chopped parsley
- 4 pounds osso bucco

Instructions

Put all ingredients in the slow cooker and cook on low for 8 hours.

Duck Stew

Serves 8

Ingredients - Allergies: SF, GF, DF, EF, NF

- 2 Tbsp. olive oil
- 2 pound chopped duck meat (1/2 inch wide)
- 1/2 pound duck liver, sliced
- 1 chopped carrot
- 1 cup chopped celery
- 1 small chopped onion
- 2 garlic cloves, chopped
- 2 cups chicken broth
- 1 cup sliced shiitake mushrooms
- 1/2 cup cilantro

Instructions

Put all ingredients in the slow cooker and cook on low for 4 Hrs.

Slow cooked Cauliflower Coconut Curry

Serves: 6

Ingredients - Allergies: SF, GF, NF

- Curry Paste – see recipe
- 2 cups thick coconut milk
- 3 tbsp. coconut oil
- 1 tomato
- 3 cups chopped Cauliflower
- 1/2 cup chopped Green Peppers
- Cilantro for topping

Instructions

Put all ingredients in the slow cooker and cook on low for 4 Hrs.

Pork, Celery and Basil Stew

Serves 8

Ingredients - Allergies: SF, GF, DF, EF, NF

- 1 small chopped onion
- 2 Tbsp. coconut oil
- 2 1/2 pounds chopped pork meat
- 1 chopped carrot
- 2 cups beef stock
- Salt
- Black pepper
- 1 bunch chopped parsley
- 1 cup chopped celery
- 1/2 cup fresh basil

Instructions

Add all ingredients to slow cooker and cook on low for 8 hours.

Pork Tenderloin with peppers and onions
Serves 3-4

Ingredients - Allergies: SF, GF, DF, EF, NF

- 1 tbsp. coconut oil
- 1 pound pork loin
- 1 tbsp. caraway seeds
- 1/2 tsp sea salt
- 1/4 tsp black pepper
- 1 small onion, thinly sliced
- 1 red bell pepper, sliced
- 2 cloves of garlic, minced
- 1/4-1/3 cup chicken broth

Instructions

Wash and chop vegetables. Slice pork loin, and season with black pepper, caraway seeds and sea salt. Heat a pan over medium heat. Add coconut oil when hot. Add pork loin and brown slightly. Add onions and mushrooms, and continue to sauté until onions are translucent. Add peppers, garlic and chicken broth. Simmer until vegetables are tender and pork is fully cooked.

Beef Bourguinon

Serves 8-10

Ingredients - Allergies: SF, GF, DF, EF

- 4 pounds cubed lean beef
- 1/3 cup coconut oil
- 1 tsp. thyme
- 1 tsp. black pepper
- 2 cloves garlic, crushed
- 1 small onion, diced
- 1 pound mushrooms, sliced
- 1/4 cup almond flour

Instructions

Marinate beef in wine, oil, thyme and pepper for few hours at room temperature or 6-8 hours in the fridge. Add beef with marinade and all other ingredients to a crock pot. Cook on low for 7-9 hrs.

Italian Chicken

Serves 6-8

Ingredients - Allergies: SF, GF, DF, EF

- 1 skinless chicken, cut into pieces
- 1/4 cup almond flour
- 1 1/2 tsp. salt
- 1/8 tsp. pepper
- 1/2 cup chicken broth
- 1 cup sliced mushrooms
- 1/2 tsp. paprika
- 1 zucchini, sliced into medium pieces
- black pepper
- parsley to garnish

Instructions

Season chicken with 1 tsp. salt. Combine flour, pepper, remaining salt, and paprika. Coat chicken pieces with this mixture. Place zucchini first in a crockpot. Pour broth over zucchini. Arrange chicken on top. Cover and cook on low for 6 to 8 hours or until tender. Turn control to high, add mushrooms, cover, and cook on high for additional 10-15 minutes. Garnish with parsley and black pepper.

Ropa Vieja

Ingredients - Allergies: SF, GF, DF, EF, NF

6 servings

- 1 tbsp. coconut oil
- 2 pounds beef flank steak
- 1 cup beef broth
- 1 small onion, sliced
- 1 green bell pepper sliced into strips
- 2 cloves garlic, chopped
- 1 tsp. ground cumin
- 1 tsp. chopped cilantro
- 1 tbsp. olive oil & 1 tbsp. lemon juice

Instructions

Add all ingredients to a crock pot. Cover, and cook on high for 4 hours, or on Low for up to 8 hours.

Lemon Roast Chicken

Serves 6-8

Ingredients - Allergies: SF, GF, DF, EF, NF

- 1 whole skinless chicken
- 1 dash Salt
- 1 dash Pepper
- 1 tsp. Oregano
- 2 cloves minced garlic
- 2 tbsp. coconut oil
- 1/4 cup Water
- 3 tbsp. Lemon juice
- Rosemary

Instructions

Add ingredients to a crock pot and cover. Cook on low 7 hours. Add lemon juice when cooking is done.

Red Peppers Pork Curry

Serves 8

Ingredients - Allergies: SF, GF, DF, EF, NF

- 1 cup sliced red peppers
- 1 small chopped onion
- 2 tbsp. coconut oil
- 1 cup curry paste*
- 4 pounds cubed pork meat

Instructions

Put ingredients in the slow cooker. Cover, and cook on low for 7 to 9 hours.

Beef Ratatouille

Serves 8

Ingredients - Allergies: SF, GF, DF, EF, NF

- 1 cup sliced zucchini
- 1 small chopped onion
- 1/2 cup sliced eggplant
- ½ cup sliced red peppers
- 2 tbsp. coconut oil
- 2 tbsp. minced garlic
- 2 tsp. salt and 1 tsp. ground pepper
- 4 pounds cubed beef

Instructions

Put ingredients in the slow cooker. Cover, and cook on low for 7 to 9 hours.

Crock Pot Turkey Roast Mediterranean style

Serves 8

Ingredients - Allergies: SF, GF, DF, EF, NF

- 1/2 cup Kalamata olives
- 1/4 cup chopped sun dried tomatoes
- 1 cup chicken broth
- 2 garlic cloves, minced
- 1 small chopped onion
- 2 tbsp. coconut oil
- 4 pounds turkey breast
- Rub thyme, salt and black pepper.

Instructions

Put ingredients in the slow cooker. Cover, and cook on low for 7 to 9 hours.

Slow Cooker Pot Roast

Serves 8

Ingredients - Allergies: SF, GF, DF, EF, NF

- 2 cups sliced celery
- 1 chopped carrot
- 3 cups beef broth
- 2 garlic cloves, minced
- 1 small chopped onion
- 2 tbsp. coconut oil
- 4 pounds beef chuck roast
- Rub thyme, salt and black pepper. Add 1 bay leaf.

Instructions

Put ingredients in the slow cooker. Cover, and cook on low for 7 to 9 hours.

Crock Pot Whole Chicken
Serves 8

Ingredients - Allergies: SF, GF, DF, EF, NF

- 2 cup sliced celery
- 1 chopped carrot
- 1 small chopped onion
- 2 tbsp. coconut oil
- 1 whole chicken with skin on
- Rub paprika, salt and black pepper on the chicken skin and inside. Optionally add lemon quarters inside.

Instructions

Put veggies in the slow cooker and place chicken on top. Cover, and cook on low for 7 to 9 hours.

Beef, Leeks & Mushrooms Stew

Serves 8

Ingredients - Allergies: SF, GF, DF, EF, NF

- 1 chopped carrot
- 2 tbsp. coconut oil
- 1/2 cup chopped leeks
- Salt & black pepper to taste
- 1 cup sliced mushrooms
- 4 pounds beef meat cut into stripes

Instructions

Put ingredients in the slow cooker. Cover, and cook on low for 7 to 9 hours.

Minced Pork, Tomato & Red Peppers Stew
Serves 8

Ingredients - Allergies: SF, GF, DF, EF, NF

- 1 sliced tomato
- 1 small chopped onion
- 2 tbsp. coconut oil
- 1/2 cup chopped red peppers
- Salt, black pepper and ground cumin to taste
- 1 shredded carrot
- 1 Tsp. paprika
- 4 pounds minced pork meat

Instructions

Put ingredients in the slow cooker. Cover, and cook on low for 7 to 9 hours.

Beef, Eggplant & Celery Stew

Serves 8

Ingredients - Allergies: SF, GF, DF, EF, NF

- 1 cup cubed eggplant
- 1 small chopped onion
- 2 tbsp. coconut oil
- 2 cups sliced celery
- Salt, black pepper to taste
- 4 pounds beef meat cut into stripes

Instructions

Put ingredients in the slow cooker. Cover, and cook on low for 7 to 9 hours.

Beef Pot Roast with Broccoli

Serves 8

Ingredients - Allergies: SF, GF, DF, EF, NF

- 1 small chopped onion
- 2 tbsp. coconut oil
- 3 cups broccoli
- Salt, black pepper & 2 bay leaves
- 2 cups beef stock
- 2 tsp. minced garlic
- 4 pounds beef pot roast

Instructions

Put ingredients in the slow cooker. Cover, and cook on low for 7 to 9 hours.

Mixed Seafood & Saffron Stew

Serves 8

Ingredients - Allergies: SF, GF, DF, EF, NF

- 1/4 cup sundried tomatoes (optional)
- 1 small chopped onion
- 2 tbsp. coconut oil
- 1/4 cup olive oil mixed with 1 tsp. saffron
- Salt
- 2 cups vegetable or fish broth
- 4 pounds frozen mixed seafood

Instructions

Put ingredients in the slow cooker. Cover, and cook on high for 90 minutes.

Jerk Chicken

Serves 8

Ingredients - Allergies: SF, GF, DF, EF, NF

- 1 sliced green peppers
- 1 small chopped onion
- 2 tbsp. coconut oil
- Salt, black pepper and ground allspice to taste
- 2 cups chicken stock
- 4 pounds cubed chicken meat
- 1 lime - juice & 1 or more Scotch bonnet peppers (to taste).
- 2 Tbsp. minced ginger & 2 Tsp. minced garlic.
- 1/4 Tsp. cinnamon & a pinch of nutmeg.

Instructions

Put ingredients in the slow cooker. Cover, and cook on low for 8 hours.

Cauliflower Beef & Carrot

Serves 8

Ingredients - Allergies: SF, GF, DF, EF, NF

- 1 chopped carrot
- 1 chopped red onion
- 2 tbsp. coconut oil
- 2 cups cauliflower florets
- 1 cup chopped celery
- Salt, black pepper and ground cumin to taste
- 2 cups beef stock
- 4 pounds cubed beef meat

Instructions

Put ingredients in the slow cooker. Cover, and cook on low for 7 to 9 hours.

Pork Broccoli

Serves 8

Ingredients - Allergies: SF, GF, DF, EF, NF

- 1 small chopped onion
- 2 tbsp. coconut oil
- 3 cups broccoli
- Salt, black pepper and 1 Tbsp. chopped garlic
- 2 cups beef stock
- 4 pounds Pork roast

Instructions

Put ingredients in the slow cooker. Cover, and cook on low for 7 to 9 hours.

Pork & Leeks

Serves 8

Ingredients - Allergies: SF, GF, DF, EF, NF

- 1 chopped carrot
- 2 tbsp. coconut oil
- 1 cup chopped leeks
- Salt, black pepper and ground cumin to taste
- 2 cups beef stock
- 4 pounds cubed pork meat

Instructions

Put ingredients in the slow cooker. Cover, and cook on low for 7 to 9 hours.

Italian Beef

Serves 8

Ingredients - Allergies: SF, GF, DF, EF, NF

- 1 red pepper, sliced
- 1 small chopped onion
- 2 tbsp. coconut oil
- Salt, black pepper and ground cumin to taste
- 2 bay leaves, 2 Tsp. chopped garlic, 1 tsp. oregano, dried basil and dried parsley each (optional)
- 2 cups beef stock
- 4 pounds beef chuck (rump) roast

Instructions

Put ingredients in the slow cooker. Cover, and cook on low for 9 hours.

Salmon &Mushrooms

Serves 8

Ingredients - Allergies: SF, GF, DF, EF, NF

- 3 cups sliced mushrooms
- 1 small chopped onion
- 2 tbsp. coconut oil
- Salt, black pepper
- 4 pounds cubed salmon

Instructions

Put ingredients in the slow cooker. Cover, and cook on low for 2.5-3 Hrs.

Mustard Chicken

Serves 8

Ingredients - Allergies: SF, GF, DF, EF, NF

- 1 cup chopped leeks
- 2 cups chopped mushrooms
- 2 tbsp. coconut oil
- Salt, black pepper
- 2 Tbsp. Mustard seeds (white and brown or black seeds)
- 1 cup chicken stock (3 cups if adding optional rice)
- 4 pounds cubed chicken meat

Instructions

Put ingredients in the slow cooker. Cover, and cook on low for 7 to 9 hours.

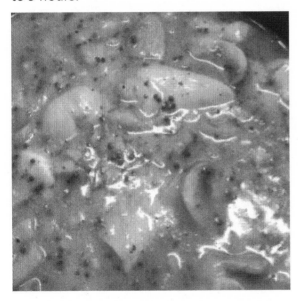

Eggplant, Tripe & Broccoli

Serves 8

Ingredients - Allergies: SF, GF, DF, EF, NF

- 1 cup eggplant, cubed
- 1 small chopped onion
- 3 cups broccoli
- 2 tbsp. coconut oil
- Salt, black pepper,
- 2 bay leaves & 2 Tsp. chopped garlic
- 3 cups beef stock
- 4 pounds beef tripe cut into stripes

Instructions

Put ingredients in the slow cooker. Cover, and cook on low for 9 hours.

Cauliflower and Minced Beef

Serves 8

Ingredients - Allergies: SF, GF, DF, EF, NF

- 1 chopped tomato
- 4 cups cauliflower florets
- 1 small chopped onion
- 2 tbsp. coconut oil
- Salt, black pepper and cumin to taste
- 2 bay leaves & 2 Tsp. chopped garlic & 1 tsp. oregano
- 3 cups beef stock
- 4 pounds minced beef

Instructions

Put ingredients in the slow cooker. Cover, and cook on low for 9 hours.

Kare Kare – oxtail stew

Serves 8

Ingredients - Allergies: SF, GF, DF, EF, NF

- 2 cups broccoli
- 1 small chopped onion
- 2 tbsp. coconut oil
- Salt, black pepper and ground cumin to taste
- 2 bay leaves & 2 Tsp. chopped garlic
- 2 cups beef stock
- 4 pounds oxtail cut into 2 inch chunks

Instructions

Put ingredients in the slow cooker. Cover, and cook on low for 9 hours.

Osso Bucco with shredded veggies

Serves 8

Ingredients - Allergies: SF, GF, DF, EF, NF

- 1/2 cup shredded carrots
- 1/2 cup chopped leeks
- 2 cups chopped celery
- Salt, black pepper to taste
- 2 bay leaves & 2 Tbsp. chopped garlic
- 2 cups beef stock
- 4 pounds veal osso bucco

Instructions

Mix all veggies and spices and put half at the bottom of the slow cooker dish. Put osso bucco on top, add the rest of the mix and pour liquid. Cover, and cook on low for 9 hours.

Leeks, Mushrooms & Pork Neck Meat

Serves 8

Ingredients - Allergies: SF, GF, DF, EF, NF

- 3 cups mushrooms, sliced
- 1/4 cups chopped leeks
- 2 tbsp. coconut oil
- Salt, black pepper and ground cumin to taste
- 2 bay leaves & 2 Tsp. chopped garlic
- 4 cups beef stock
- ¼ cup sesame seeds
- 1/4 cup chopped spring onions
- 4 pounds pork neck meat

Instructions

Put all ingredients in the slow cooker except spring onions and sesame seeds. Cover, and cook on low for 9 hours. Sprinkle with chopped spring onions and sesame seeds.

Beef, Beet, Carrots & Onions

Serves 8

Ingredients - Allergies: SF, GF, DF, EF, NF

- 1/2 cup julienned carrots
- 1/2 cup beets, peeled and sliced
- 1 small chopped onion
- 2 tbsp. coconut oil
- Salt, black pepper to taste
- 2 cups beef stock
- 4 pounds cubed beef
- 1 Tsp. minced garlic.

Instructions

Put ingredients in the slow cooker. Cover, and cook on low for 8 hours.

Broccoli, Pork & Peppers

Serves 8

Ingredients - Allergies: SF, GF, DF, EF, NF

- 1 sliced yellow and orange pepper
- 1 small chopped onion
- 2 tbsp. coconut oil
- Salt, black pepper to taste
- 1 cup beef stock
- 2 pounds pork chops
- 2 pounds pork neck
- 1 Tsp. minced garlic.
- 2 cups broccoli florets

Instructions

Put ingredients in the slow cooker. Cover, and cook on low for 8 hours.

Haitian Chicken Broccoli

Serves 8

Ingredients - Allergies: SF, GF, DF, EF, NF

- 3 cup broccoli florets
- 1 small chopped onion
- 2 tbsp. coconut oil
- Salt, black pepper to taste
- 3 cups chicken stock
- 4 pounds cubed chicken meat
- 1 tsp. dried red pepper flakes (to taste).
- 4 whole cloves (discard after cooking)
- 2 Tsp. minced garlic
- 1 Tsp. apple vinegar

Instructions

Put ingredients in the slow cooker. Cover, and cook on low for 8 hours.

Bok Choy, Cauliflower, Chicken & Carrot

Serves 8

Ingredients - Allergies: SF, GF, DF, EF, NF

- 3 cups sliced bok choy
- 1 sliced carrot
- 2 tbsp. coconut oil
- Salt, black pepper to taste
- 2 cups chicken stock
- 4 pounds cubed chicken meat
- 2 Tsp. minced ginger & 2 Tsp. minced garlic.
- 2 sticks celery, chopped

Instructions

Put ingredients in the slow cooker. Cover, and cook on low for 8 hours.

Okra & Pork Stew

Serves 8

Ingredients - Allergies: SF, GF, DF, EF, NF

- 3 cups sliced okra
- 1 small chopped onion
- 2 tbsp. coconut oil
- Salt, black pepper to taste
- 2 cups beef stock
- 4 pounds pork neck meat
- 2 cloves garlic, halved lengthwise
- 2 sticks celery, chopped

Instructions

Put ingredients in the slow cooker. Cover, and cook on low for 8 hours.

Celery, Carrots & Cauliflower Pork

Serves 8

Ingredients - Allergies: SF, GF, DF, EF, NF

- 2 cups sliced celery
- 1 small chopped onion
- 2 tbsp. coconut oil
- Salt, black pepper to taste
- 2 cups beef stock
- 4 pounds cubed pork meat
- 1 chopped carrot
- 2 cups chopped cauliflower
- 2 Tbsp. minced garlic & 3-4 bay leaves (discard after cooking).

Instructions

Put ingredients in the slow cooker. Cover, and cook on low for 8 hours.

Slow Cooked Carnitas

Serves 8

Ingredients - Allergies: SF, GF, DF, EF, NF

- 1 small chopped onion
- 2 tbsp. coconut oil
- Salt, black pepper to taste
- 2 pounds pork shoulder
- 2 pounds pork neck
- 1 Jalapeno pepper, chopped (to taste).
- 2 Tsp. minced garlic.
- 1 Tbsp. ground cumin.

Instructions

Put ingredients in the slow cooker. Cover, and cook on low for 8 hours.

Bigos- Polish Pork, Venison & Cabbage Stew

Serves 8

Ingredients - Allergies: SF, GF, DF, EF, NF

- 1 small chopped onion
- 2 tbsp. coconut oil
- Salt, black pepper to taste
- 2 pound pork shoulder meat, cubed
- 2 pounds venison meat, cubed
- 3 cups shredded cabbage
- 2 Tsp. minced garlic
- 1 Tsp. ground paprika

Instructions

Put ingredients in the slow cooker. Cover, and cook on low for 8 hours.

Cumin Lamb

Serves 8

Ingredients - Allergies: SF, GF, DF, EF, NF

- 1 small chopped onion
- 2 tbsp. coconut oil
- Salt, black pepper to taste
- 4 pounds lamb meat, cubed
- 1 cup parsley
- 1/2 cup sesame seeds
- 2 Tsp. minced garlic
- 3 Tsp. ground cumin

Instructions

Put ingredients in the slow cooker. Cover, and cook on low for 8 hours.

Moroccan Lamb, Celery & Green Peppers Stew
Serves 8

Ingredients - Allergies: SF, GF, DF, EF, NF

- 1 small chopped onion
- 2 tbsp. coconut oil
- Salt, black pepper to taste
- 4 pounds lamb meat, cubed
- 2 cups beef broth
- 2 green peppers, sliced
- 2 cups celery, sliced
- 2 Tsp. minced garlic.
- 2 Tsp. ground cumin.

Instructions

Put ingredients in the slow cooker. Cover, and cook on low for 8 hours.

Pork, Mushrooms & Herbs Stew

Serves 8

Ingredients - Allergies: SF, GF, DF, EF, NF

- 1 small chopped onion
- 2 tbsp. coconut oil
- Salt, black pepper to taste
- 4 pounds pork shoulder
- 3 cups sliced mushrooms
- 1/2 cup each parsley, cilantro and dill
- 2 Tsp. minced garlic.

Instructions

Put ingredients in the slow cooker. Cover, and cook on low for 8 hours.

Chicken & Artichoke Hearts

Serves 8

Ingredients - Allergies: SF, GF, DF, EF, NF

- 1 small chopped onion
- 2 tbsp. coconut oil
- Salt, black pepper to taste
- 4 pounds chicken meat
- 1 chopped carrot
- 4 medium Artichokes, tops sliced, trimmed
- 1 Tsp. ground cumin.
- 1 cup chicken broth

Instructions

Put ingredients in the slow cooker. Cover, and cook on low for 8 hours.

Green Peppers, Chicken and Green Onions

Serves 8

Ingredients - Allergies: SF, GF, DF, EF, NF

- 1/2 cup chopped green onions
- 2 tbsp. coconut oil
- Salt, black pepper to taste
- 4 pounds chopped chicken meat
- 1 cup sliced green peppers
- 2 Tsp. minced garlic.
- 1 Tsp. ground cumin.

Instructions

Put ingredients in the slow cooker. Cover, and cook on low for 8 hours.

Haitian Spinach Shrimp Stew

Serves 8

Ingredients - Allergies: SF, GF, DF, EF, NF

- 1 small chopped onion
- 2 tbsp. coconut oil
- Salt, black pepper to taste
- 4 pounds shrimp
- 3 cups spinach leaves
- 1 tsp. dried red pepper flakes (to taste).
- 4 whole cloves (discard after cooking)
- 2 cups fish broth
- 1 small tomato, sliced
- 1 lime – juice only & 1/8 ground cloves

Instructions

Put ingredients in the slow cooker. Cover, and cook on low for 8 hours.

Duck Curry

Serves 8

Ingredients - Allergies: SF, GF, DF, EF, NF

- 1 small chopped onion
- 1 chopped carrot
- 1 zucchini, sliced in 2 inch slices
- 2 tbsp. coconut oil
- 4 pounds duck meat
- Curry Paste, but go low on the heat
- 1 tsp. paprika
- 1/2 cup coconut milk or cream
- Cilantro for garnishing

Instructions

Make Curry Paste. Add the tomato paste, chicken, veggies and the cream. Stir to combine, add to crockpot and cook on low for 8 hours.

Irish Lamb Stew

Serves 8

Ingredients - Allergies: SF, GF, DF, EF, NF

- 1 small chopped onion
- 2 tbsp. coconut oil
- Salt, black pepper to taste
- 4 pounds lamb neck meat
- 3 cups cauliflower florets
- 1 chopped carrot
- 2 cups beef broth

Instructions

Put ingredients in the slow cooker. Cover, and cook on low for 8 hours.

Pork Cauliflower Stew

Serves 8

Ingredients - Allergies: SF, GF, DF, EF, NF

- 1 small chopped onion
- 2 tbsp. coconut oil
- Salt, black pepper to taste
- 4 pounds pork neck meat
- 1/4 cup sliced green onions
- 1 chopped carrot
- 2 cups beef broth
- 3 cups cauliflower
- 1 sliced tomato

Instructions

Put ingredients in the slow cooker. Cover, and cook on low for 8 hours. Sprinkle with sliced green onions.

Bonus Chapter - Meats

Roast Chicken with Rosemary
Serves 6-8

- 1 (3 pound) whole chicken, rinsed, skinned
- salt and pepper to taste
- 1 onion, quartered
- 1/4 cup chopped rosemary

Instructions - Allergies: SF, GF, DF, EF, NF

Heat the oven to 350F. Sprinkle salt and pepper on meat. Stuff with the onion and rosemary. Place in a baking dish and bake in the preheated oven until chicken is cooked through. Depending on the size of the bird, cooking time will vary.

Carne Asada

Serves 4-6 - Allergies: SF, GF, DF, EF, NF

Marinade:

Mix together the garlic, jalapeno, cilantro, salt, and pepper to make a paste. Put the paste in a container. Add the oil, lime juice and orange juice. Shake it up to combine. Use as a marinade for beef or as a table condiment.

Instructions

Put the flank steak in a baking dish and pour the marinade over it. Refrigerate up to 8 hours.
Take the steak out of the marinade and season it on both sides with salt and pepper. Grill (or broil) the steak for 7 to 10 minutes per side, turning once, until medium-rare. Put the steak on a cutting board and allow the juices to settle (5 minutes). Thinly slice the steak across the grain.

Chicken Tikka Masala

Serves 8

Ingredients - Allergies: SF, GF, DF, EF, NF

- 5 pounds chicken pieces, skinless, bone in
- 3 tbsp. toasted paprika
- 3 tbsp. toasted ground cumin
- 1 tsp. cayenne pepper
- 2 tbsp. toasted ground coriander seed
- 2 tsp. ground turmeric
- 12 chopped cloves garlic
- 3 tbsp. chopped fresh ginger
- 2 cups yogurt
- 3/4 cup lemon juice (4 to 6 lemons)
- 1 tsp. sea salt
- 4 tbsp. coconut oil
- 1 sliced onion
- 1 cup chopped tomatoes
- 1/2 cup chopped cilantro
- 1 cup coconut cream

Instructions

Score chicken deeply at 1-inch intervals with a knife. Place chicken in a large baking dish.

Combine coriander, cumin, paprika, turmeric, and cayenne in a bowl and mix. Set aside 3 tbsp. of this spice mixture. Combine remaining 6 tbsp. spice mixture with 8 cloves garlic garlic, yogurt, 2 tbsp. ginger, 1/4 cup salt and 1/2 cup lemon juice in a large bowl and combine. Pour marinade over chicken pieces and coat every surface (use hands). Refrigerate and marinate between 4 and 8 hours, turning occasionally.

Heat coconut oil in a large pot over medium-high heat and add remaining garlic and ginger. Add onions. Cook about 10 minutes, stirring occasionally. Add reserved spice mixture and cook until fragrant, about half a minute. Scrape up any browned bits from bottom of pan and add tomatoes and half of cilantro. Simmer for 15 minutes. Let cool slightly and puree.

Stir in coconut cream and remaining one quarter cup lemon juice. Season to taste with salt and set aside until chicken is cooked.

Cook chicken on a grill or under a broiler.

Remove chicken from bone and cut into rough bite-sized chunks. Add chicken chunks to pot of sauce. Bring to a simmer over medium heat and cook about 10 minutes.
Sprinkle with remaining cilantro.

Bonus Chapter - Meatballs

Baked Beef Meatballs

This amount is for 4 servings. Adjust for 2 if you want, eat one serving, freeze one or prepare it as is for 4 servings and then freeze 3/4 for some tasty casserole recipes like "Beef Meatballs Casserole with Green Beans" or with "Beef Meatballs Casserole with Broccoli".

Allergies: SF, GF, NF

- 1 pound lean ground beef
- 2 tbsp. minced onion
- 1/2 tsp. minced garlic
- 1 tsp. parmesan cheese
- 2 eggs
- 1/2 tsp. salt
- 1/4 tsp. pepper

Mix all of the ingredients in a large bowl using your fingers. Mix until the meat no long feels slimy from the eggs. Shape in small egg size meatballs. Place on a baking sheet. Bake at 375F for 20-25 minutes until the meatballs are cooked through. Serve with large Fiber Loaded salad

Nutrition Facts

Serving Size 149 g

Amount Per Serving

Calories 268	Calories from Fat 97

	% Daily Value*
Total Fat 10.8g	**17%**
Saturated Fat 4.3g	**22%**
Trans Fat 0.0g	
Cholesterol 188mg	**63%**
Sodium 461mg	**19%**
Potassium 497mg	**14%**
Total Carbohydrates 1.1g	**0%**
Protein 39.5g	

Vitamin A 3%	•	Vitamin C 1%
Calcium 8%	•	Iron 121%

Nutrition Grade B
* Based on a 2000 calorie diet

with Italian Dressing.

Middle Eastern Meatballs

Makes about 20 meatballs - Allergies: SF, GF, DF, EF, NF

Ingredients

- Ground lamb or beef, or a mixture of the two -- 2 pounds
- Onion, minced -- 1
- Fresh parsley or mint, finely chopped -- 1/2 bunch
- Ground cumin -- 1 tbsp.
- Cinnamon -- 2 teaspoons
- Allspice (optional) -- 1 tsp.
- Salt and pepper -- to season
- coconut oil -- 1/4 cup

Instructions

Place the ground beef or lamb, onion, herbs, spices, salt and pepper in a bowl and knead well. Chill for 1-2 hours and let the flavors mingle. Form the meat into patties or balls the size of a small egg.

Bake in the oven on 350F. Serve with tzatziki sauce.

Variations

Experiment with different seasonings--coriander, cayenne, sesame seeds.

Superfoods Reference Book

Unfortunately, I had to take out the whole Superfoods Reference Book out of all of my books because parts of that book are featured on my blog. I joined Kindle Direct Publishing Select program which allows me to have all my books free for 5 days every 3 months. Unfortunately, KDP Select program also means that all my books have to have unique content that is not available in any other online store or on the Internet (including my blog). I didn't want to remove parts of Superfoods Reference book that is already on my blog because I want that all people have free access to that information. I also wanted to be part of KDP Select program because that is an option to give my book for free to anyone. So, some sections of my Superfoods Reference Book can be found on my blog, under Superfoods menu on my blog. Complete Reference book is available for subscribers to my Superfoods Today Newsletter. Subscribers to my Newsletter will also get information whenever any of my books becomes free on Amazon. I will not offer any product pitches or anything similar to my subscribers, only Superfoods related information, recipes and weight loss and fitness tips. So, subscribe to my newsletter, download Superfoods Today Desserts free eBook which has complete Superfood Reference book included and have the opportunity to get all of my future books for free.

Your Free Gift

As a way of saying thanks for your purchase, I'm offering you my FREE eBook that is exclusive to my book and blog readers.

Superfoods Cookbook Book Two has over 70 Superfoods recipes and complements Superfoods Cookbook Book One and it contains Superfoods Salads, Superfoods Smoothies and Superfoods Deserts with ultra-healthy non-refined ingredients. All ingredients are 100% Superfoods.

It also contains Superfoods Reference book which is organized by Superfoods (more than 60 of them, with the list of their benefits), Superfoods spices, all vitamins, minerals and antioxidants. Superfoods Reference Book lists Superfoods that can help with 12 diseases and 9 types of cancer.

http://www.SuperfoodsToday.com/FREE

Other Books from this Author

Superfoods Today Diet is a Kindle Superfoods Diet book that gives you 4 week Superfoods Diet meal plan as well as 2 weeks maintenance meal plan and recipes for weight loss success. It is an extension of Detox book and it's written for people who want to switch to Superfoods lifestyle.

Superfoods Today Body Care is a Kindle book with over 50 Natural Recipes for beautiful skin and hair. It has body scrubs, facial masks and hair care recipes made with the best Superfoods like avocado honey, coconut, olive oil, oatmeal, yogurt, banana and Superfoods herbs like lavender, rosemary, mint, sage, hibiscus, rose.

Superfoods Today Cookbook is a Kindle book that contains over 160 Superfoods recipes created with 100% Superfoods ingredients. Most of the meals can be prepared in under 30 minutes and some are really quick ones that can be done in 10 minutes only. Each recipe combines Superfoods ingredients that deliver astonishing amounts of antioxidants, essential fatty acids (like omega-3), minerals, vitamins, and more.

Superfoods Today Smoothies is a Kindle Superfoods Smoothies book with over 70+ 100% Superfoods smoothies. Featured are Red, Purple, Green and Yellow Smoothies

Low Carb Recipes for Diabetics is a Kindle Superfoods <u>book</u> with Low Carb Recipes for Diabetics.

Diabetes Recipes is a Kindle Superfoods <u>book</u> with Superfoods Diabetes Recipes suitable for Diabetes Type-2.

Diabetic Cookbook for One is a Kindle Superfoods <u>book</u> with Diabetes Recipes for One suitable for Diabetes Type-2

Diabetic Meal Plans is a Kindle <u>book</u> with Superfoods Diabetes Meal Plans suitable for Diabetes Type-2

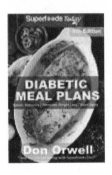

One Pot Cookbook is a Kindle Superfoods <u>book</u> with Superfoods One Pot Recipes.

Low Carb Dump Meals is a Kindle <u>book</u> with Low Carb Dump Meals Superfoods Recipes.

Superfoods Today Salads is a Kindle book that contains over 60 Superfoods Salads recipes created with 100% Superfoods ingredients. Most of the salads can be prepared in 10 minutes and most are measured for two. Each recipe combines Superfoods ingredients that deliver astonishing amounts of antioxidants, essential fatty acids (like omega-3), minerals, vitamins, and more.

Superfoods Today Kettlebells is a Kindle Kettlebells beginner's book aimed at 30+ office workers who want to improve their health and build stronger body without fat.

Superfoods Today Red Smoothies is a Kindle Superfoods Smoothies book with more than 40 Red Smoothies.

Superfoods Today 14 Days Detox is a Kindle Superfoods Detox book that gives you 2 week Superfoods Detox meal plan and recipes for Detox success.

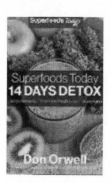

Superfoods Today Yellow Smoothies is a Kindle Superfoods Smoothies book with more than 40 Yellow Smoothies.

Superfoods Today Green Smoothies is a Kindle Superfoods Smoothies book with more than 35 Green Smoothies.

Superfoods Today Purple Smoothies is a Kindle Superfoods Smoothies book with more than 40 Purple Smoothies.

Superfoods Cooking For Two is a Kindle book that contains over 150 Superfoods recipes for two created with 100% Superfoods ingredients.

Nighttime Eater is a Kindle book that deals with Nighttime Eating Syndrome (NES). Don Orwell is a life-long Nighttime Eater that has lost his weight with Superfoods and engineered a solution around Nighttime Eating problem. Don still eats at night☺. Don't fight your nature, you can continue to eat at night, be binge free and maintain low weight.

Superfoods Today Smart Carbs 20 Days Detox is a Kindle Superfoods book that will teach you how to detox your body and start losing weight with Smart Carbs. The book has over 470+ pages with over 160+ 100% Superfoods recipes.

Superfoods Today Vegetarian Salads is a Kindle book that contains over 40 Superfoods Vegetarian Salads recipes created with 100% Superfoods ingredients. Most of the salads can be prepared in 10 minutes and most are measured for two.

Superfoods Today Vegan Salads is a Kindle book that contains over 30 Superfoods Vegan Salads recipes created with 100% Superfoods ingredients. Most of the salads can be prepared in 10 minutes and most are measured for two.

Superfoods Today Soups & Stews is a Kindle book that contains over 70 Superfoods Soups and Stews recipes created with 100% Superfoods ingredients.

Superfoods Desserts is a Kindle Superfoods Desserts book with more than 60 Superfoods Recipes.

Smoothies for Diabetics is a Kindle book that contains over 70 Superfoods Smoothies adjusted for diabetics.

50 Shades of Superfoods for Two is a Kindle book that contains over 150 Superfoods recipes for two created with 100% Superfoods ingredients.

50 Shades of Smoothies is a Kindle <u>book</u> that contains over 70 Superfoods Smoothies.

50 Shades of Superfoods Salads is a Kindle <u>book</u> that contains over 60 Superfoods Salads recipes created with 100% Superfoods ingredients. Most of the salads can be prepared in 10 minutes and most are measured for two. Each recipe combines Superfoods ingredients that deliver astonishing amounts of antioxidants, essential fatty acids (like omega-3), minerals, vitamins, and more.

Superfoods Vegan Desserts is a Kindle Vegan Dessert <u>book</u> with 100% Vegan Superfoods Recipes.

Desserts for Two is a Kindle Superfoods Desserts <u>book</u> with more than 40 Superfoods Desserts Recipes for two.

Superfoods Paleo Cookbook is a Kindle Paleo <u>book</u> with more than 150 100% Superfoods Paleo Recipes.

Superfoods Breakfasts is a Kindle Superfoods <u>book</u> with more than 40 100% Superfoods Breakfasts Recipes.

Superfoods Dump Dinners is a Kindle Superfoods book with Superfoods Dump Dinners Recipes.

Healthy Desserts is a Kindle Desserts book with more than 50 100% Superfoods Healthy Desserts Recipes.

Superfoods Salads in a Jar is a Kindle Salads in a Jar book with more than 35 100% Superfoods Salads Recipes.

Smoothies for Kids is a Kindle Smoothies book with more than 80 100% Superfoods Smoothies for Kids Recipes.

Vegan Cookbook for Beginners is a Kindle Vegan <u>book</u> with more than 75 100% Superfoods Vegan Recipes.

Vegetarian Cooking for Beginners is a Kindle Vegetarian <u>book</u> with more than 150 100% Superfoods Paleo Recipes.

Foods for Diabetics is a Kindle book with more than 170 100% Superfoods Diabetics Recipes.